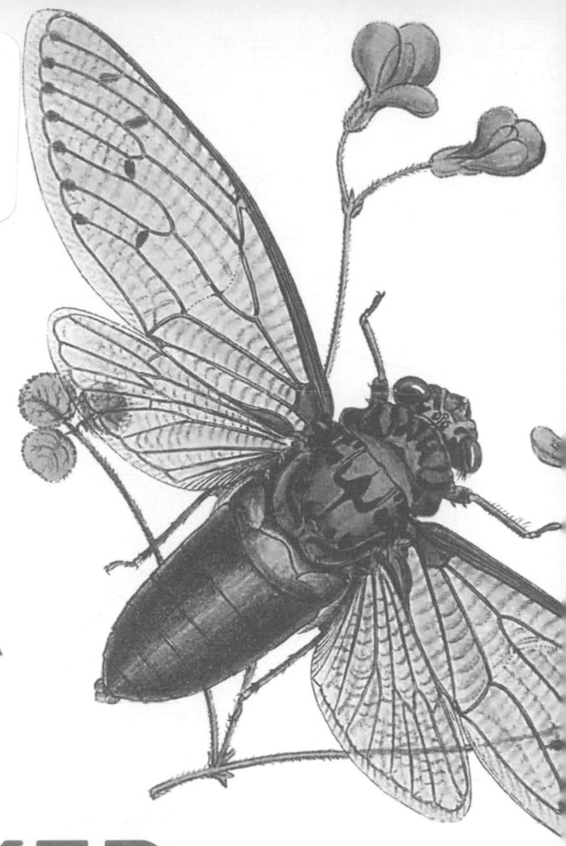

OUTDOOR SCHOOL

SPOT & STICKER
BUTTERFLIES & MOTHS

odd dot

ODD DOT • NEW YORK

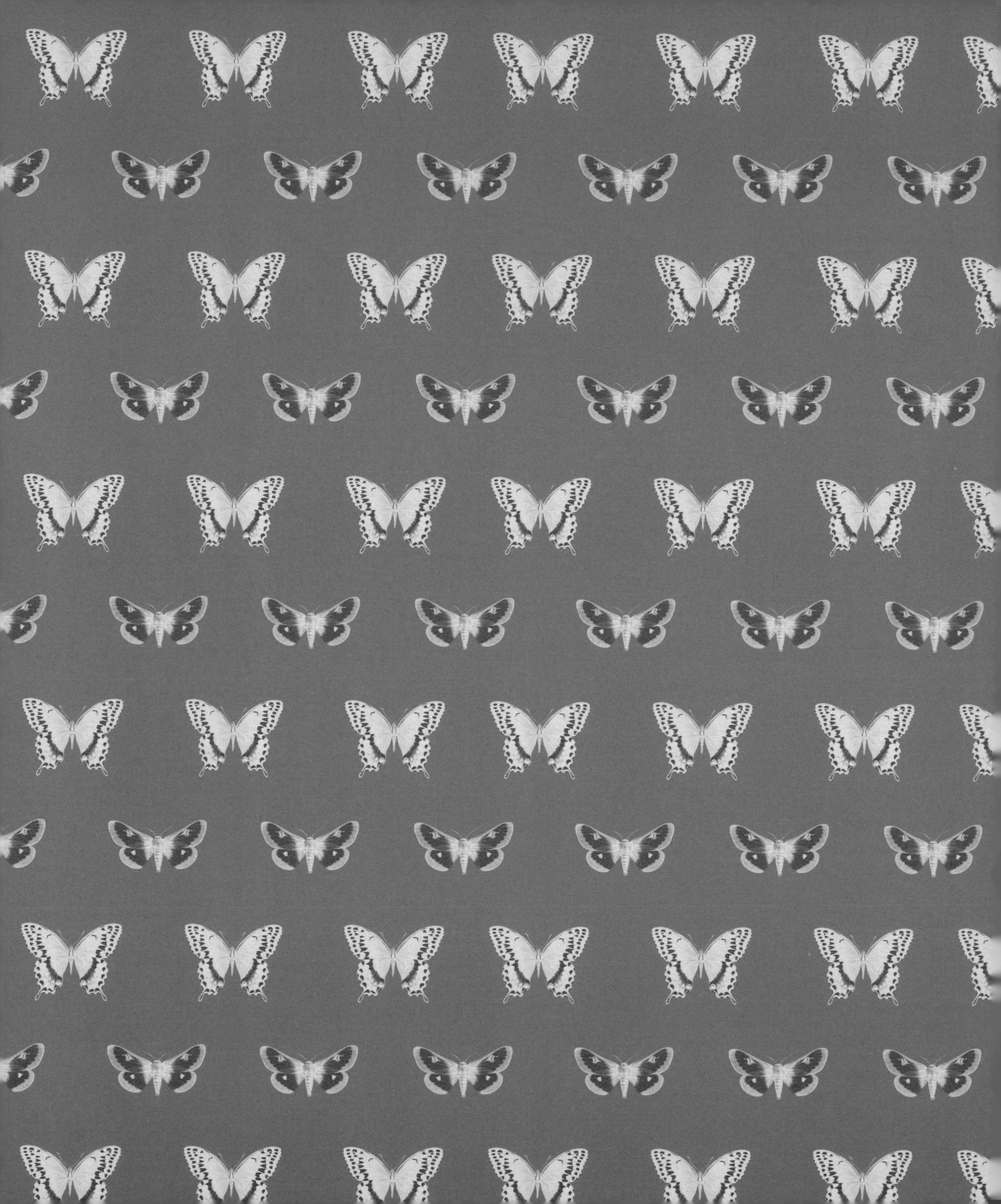

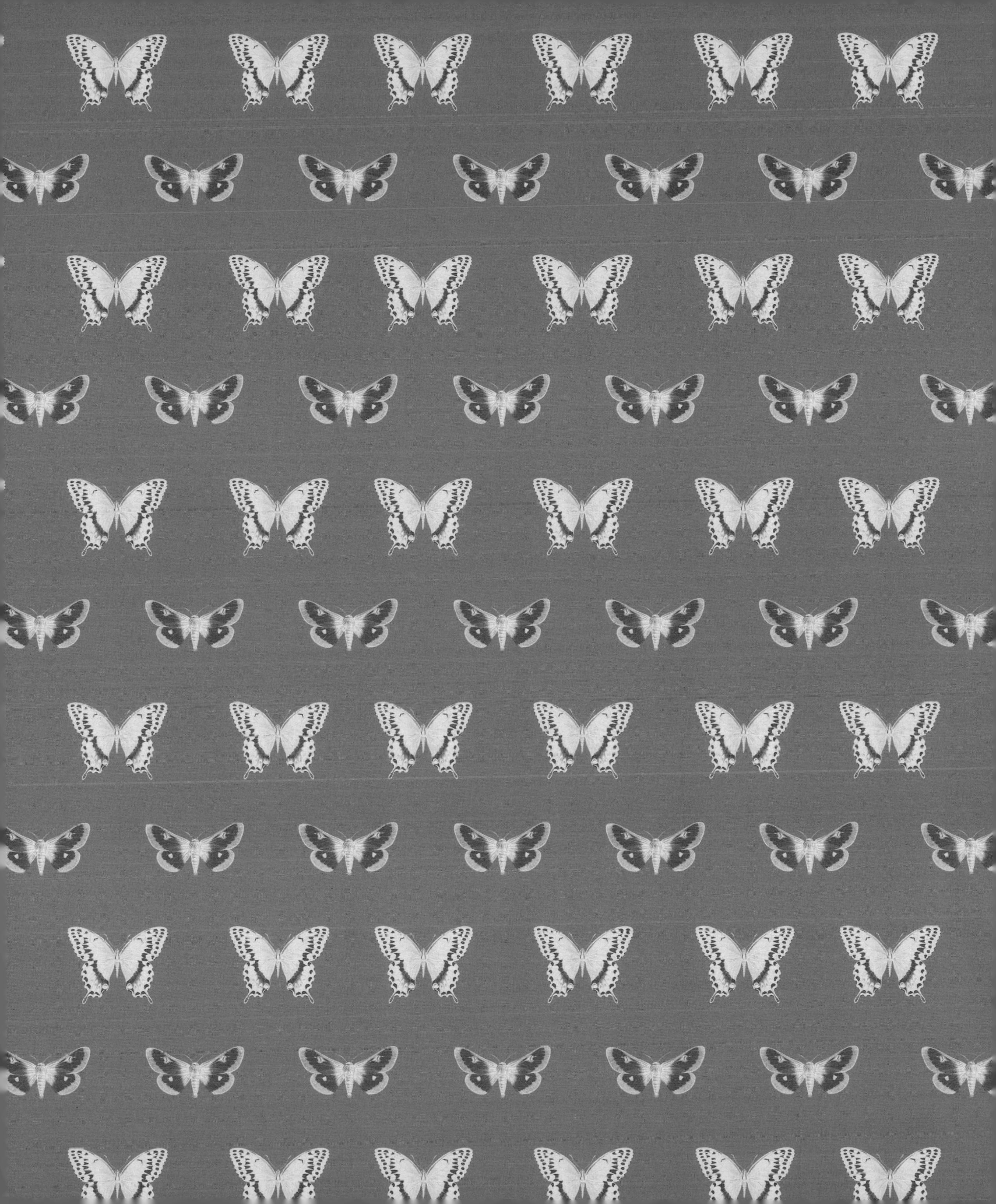

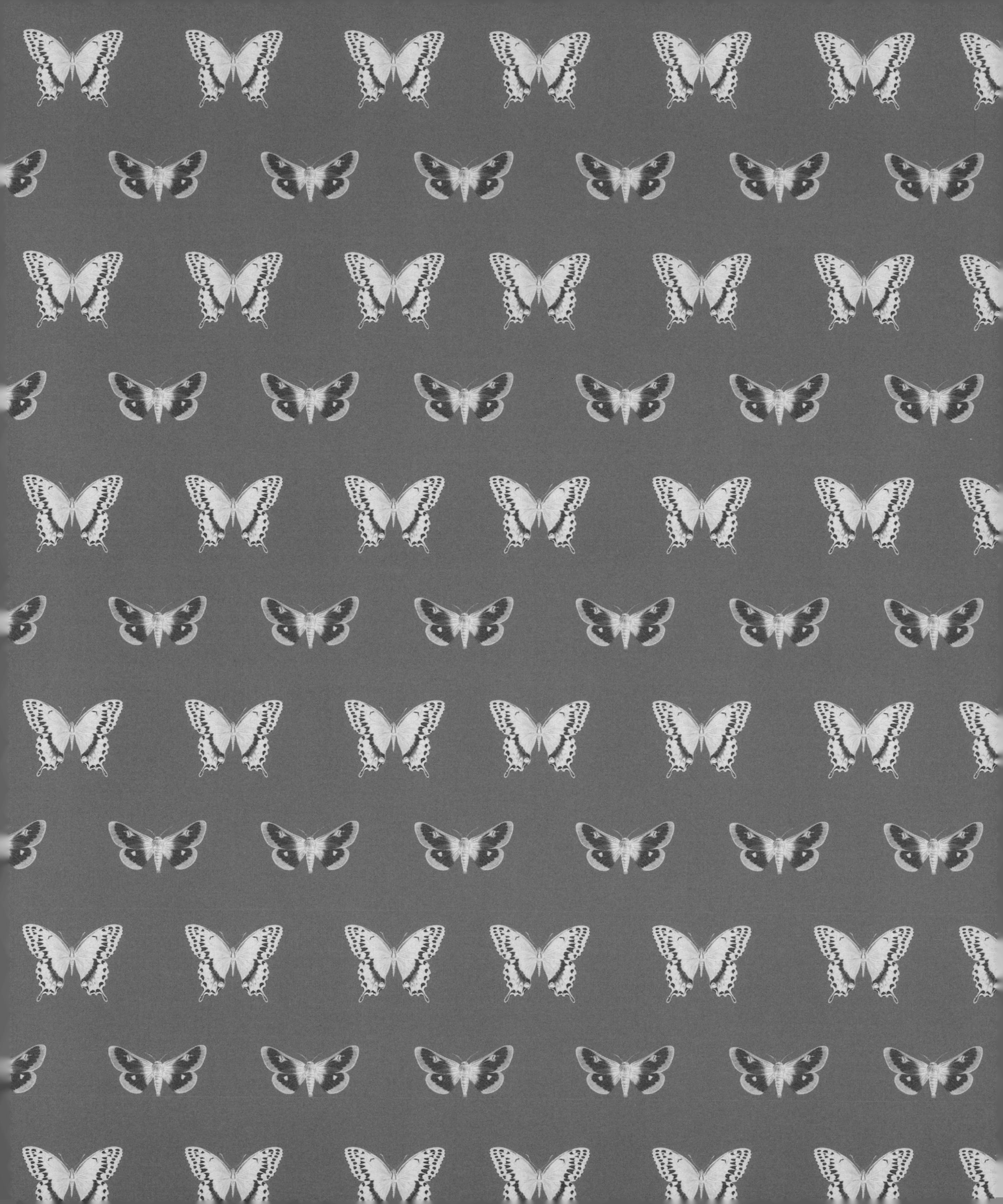

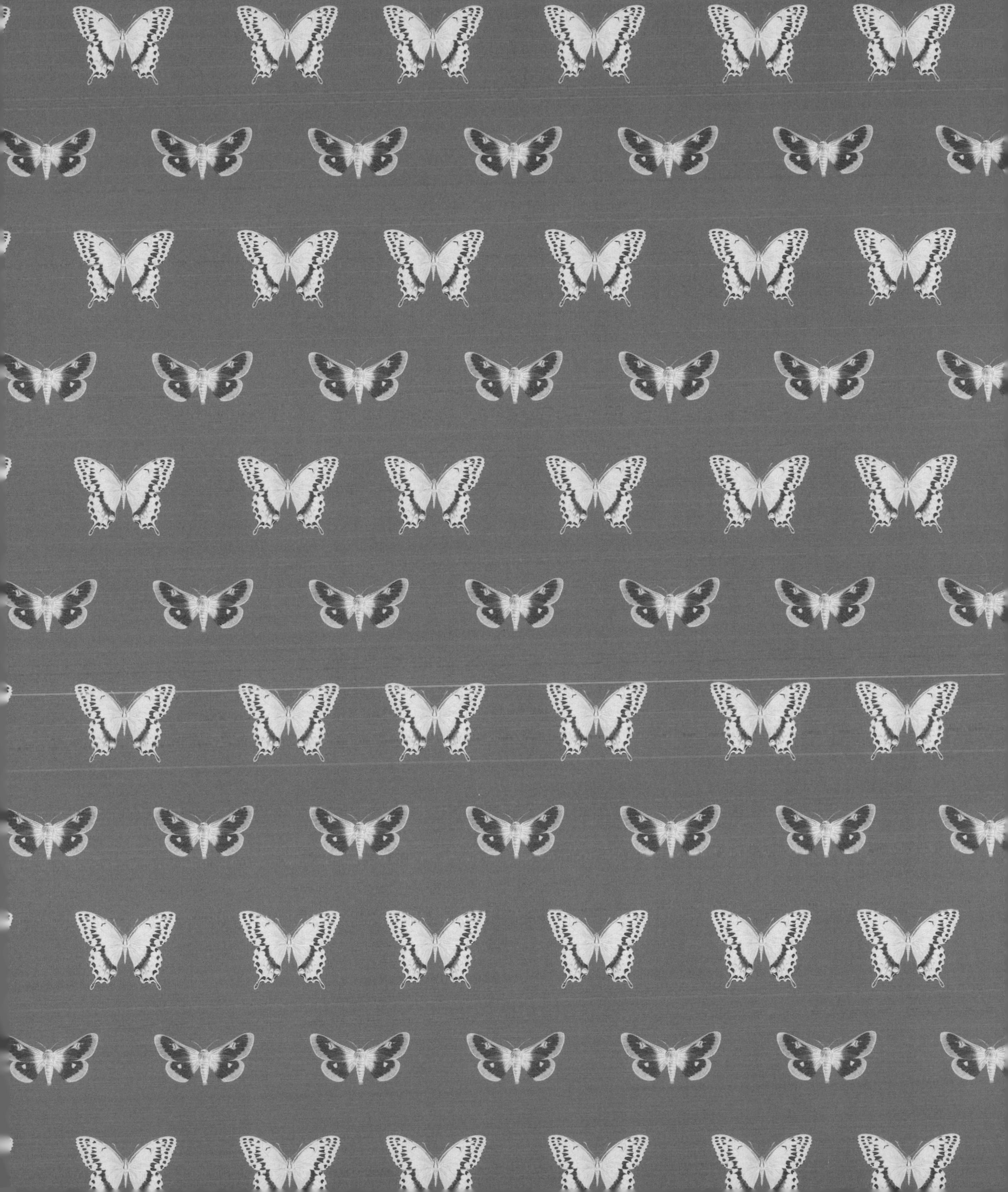

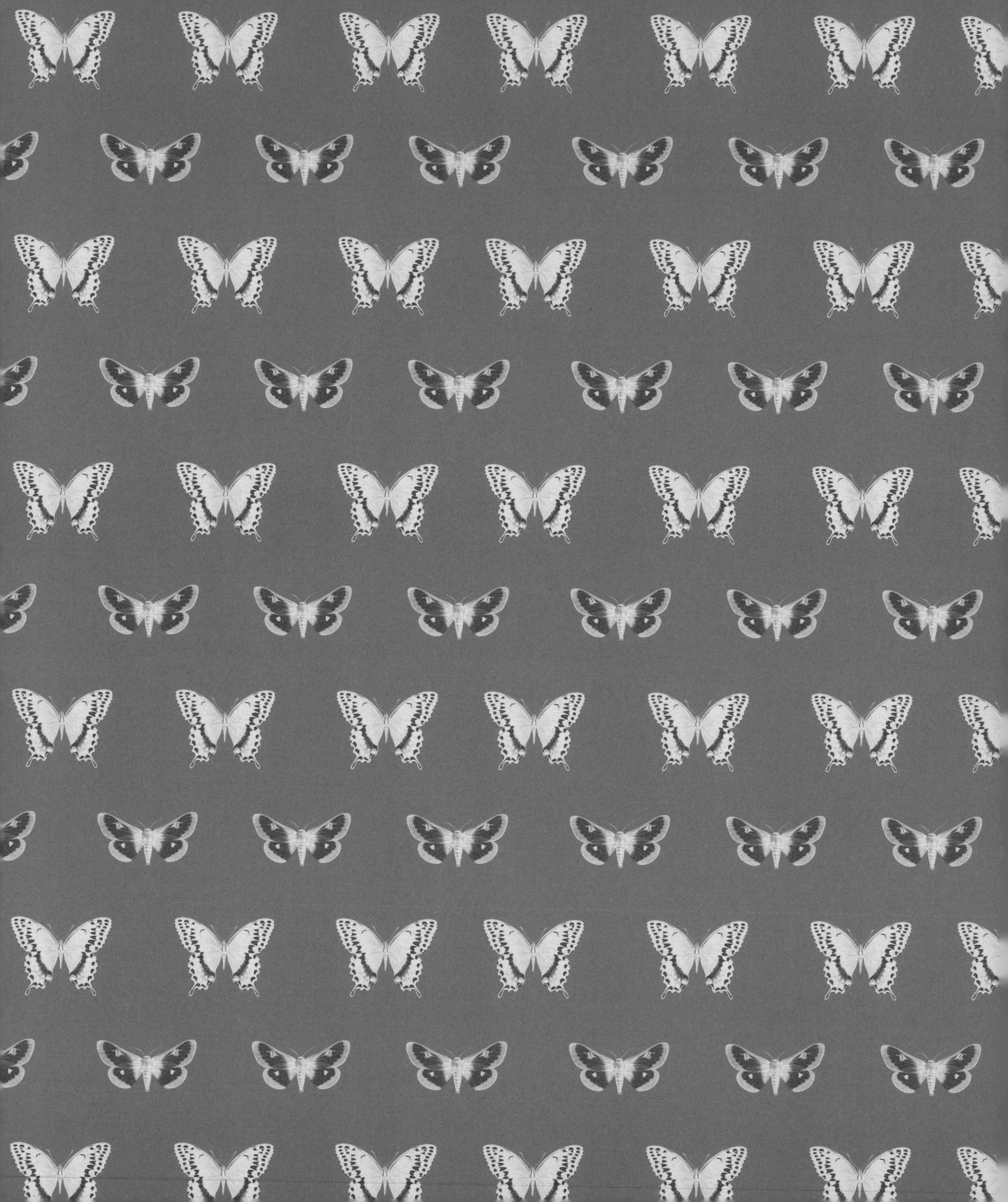

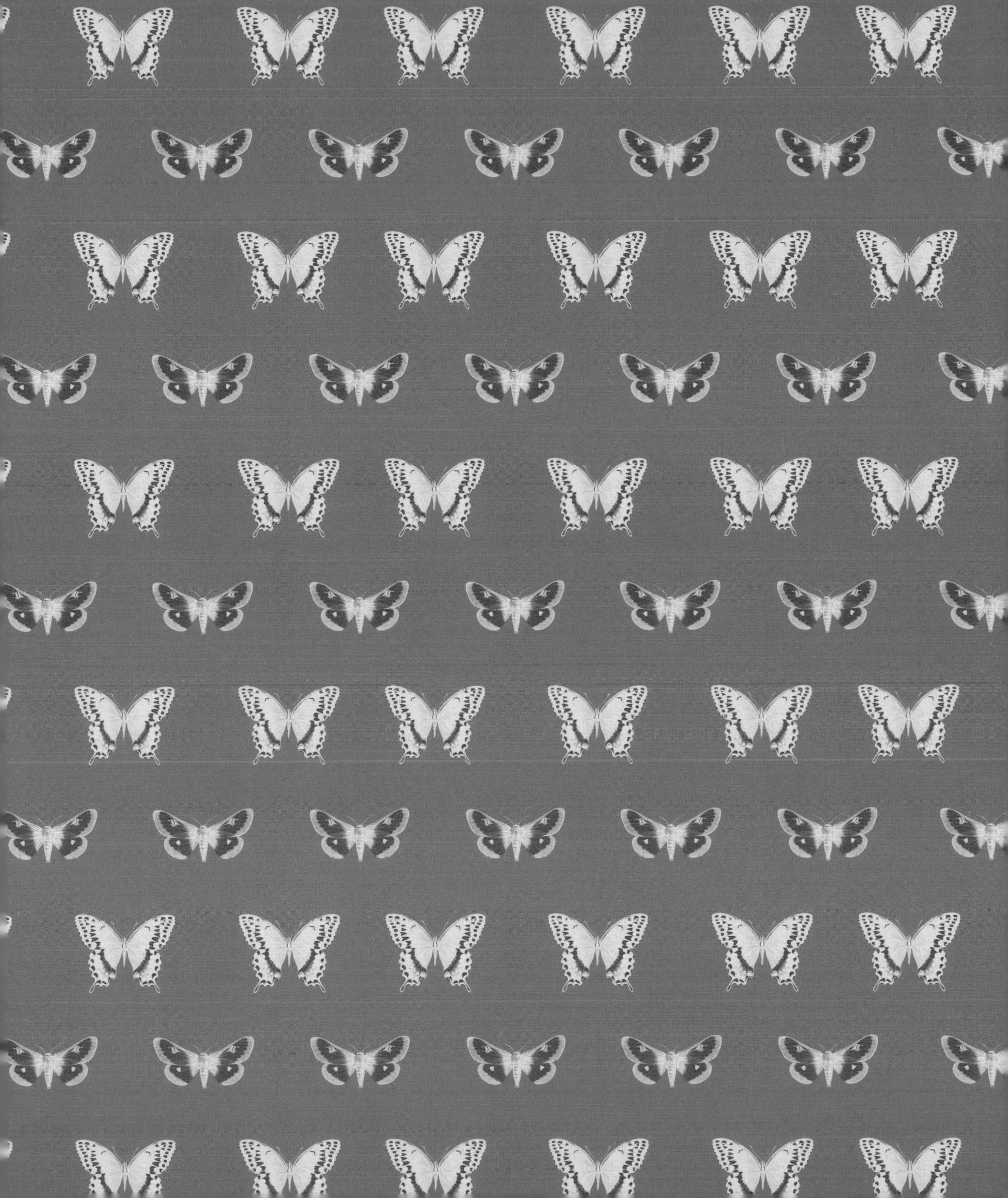

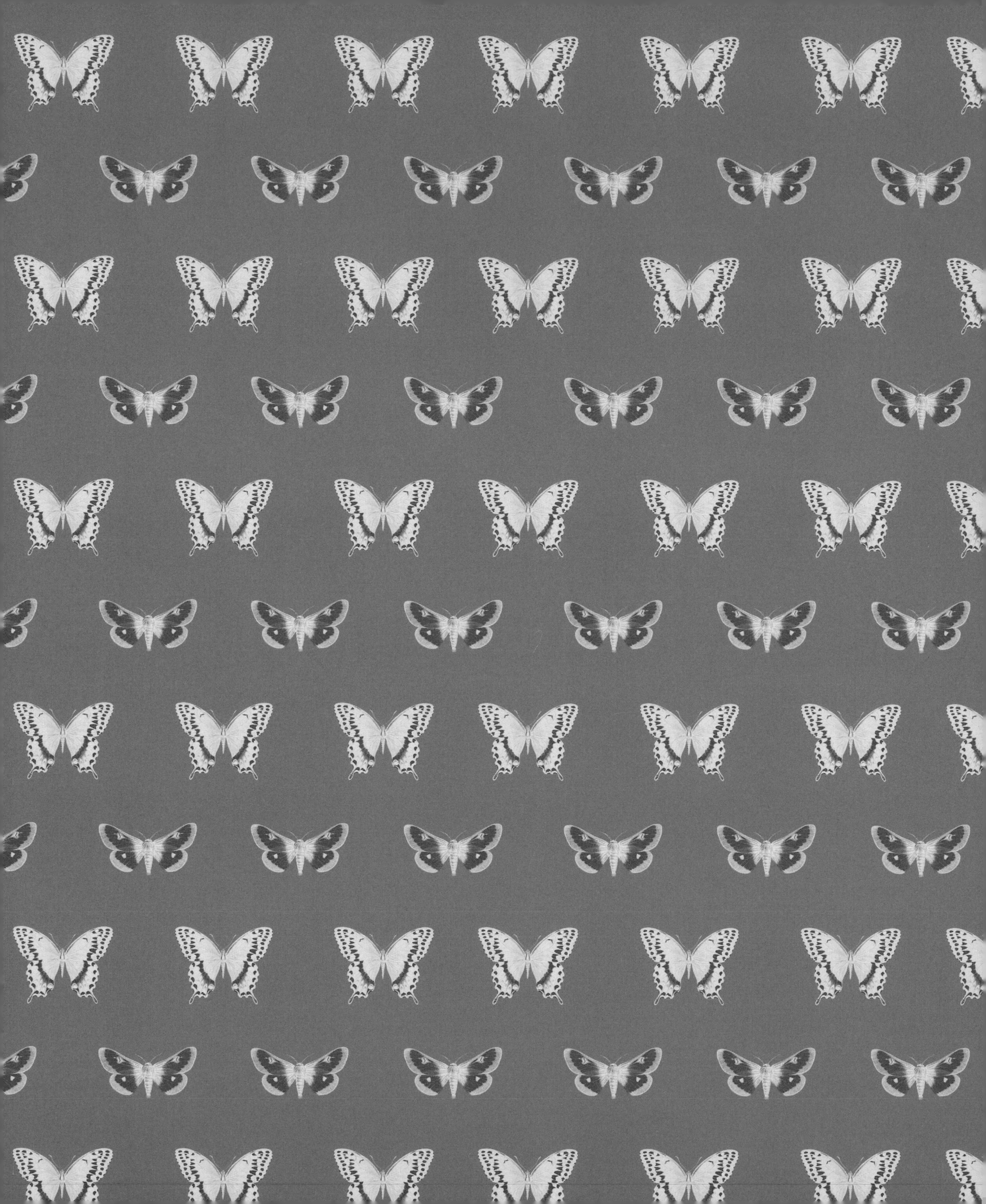

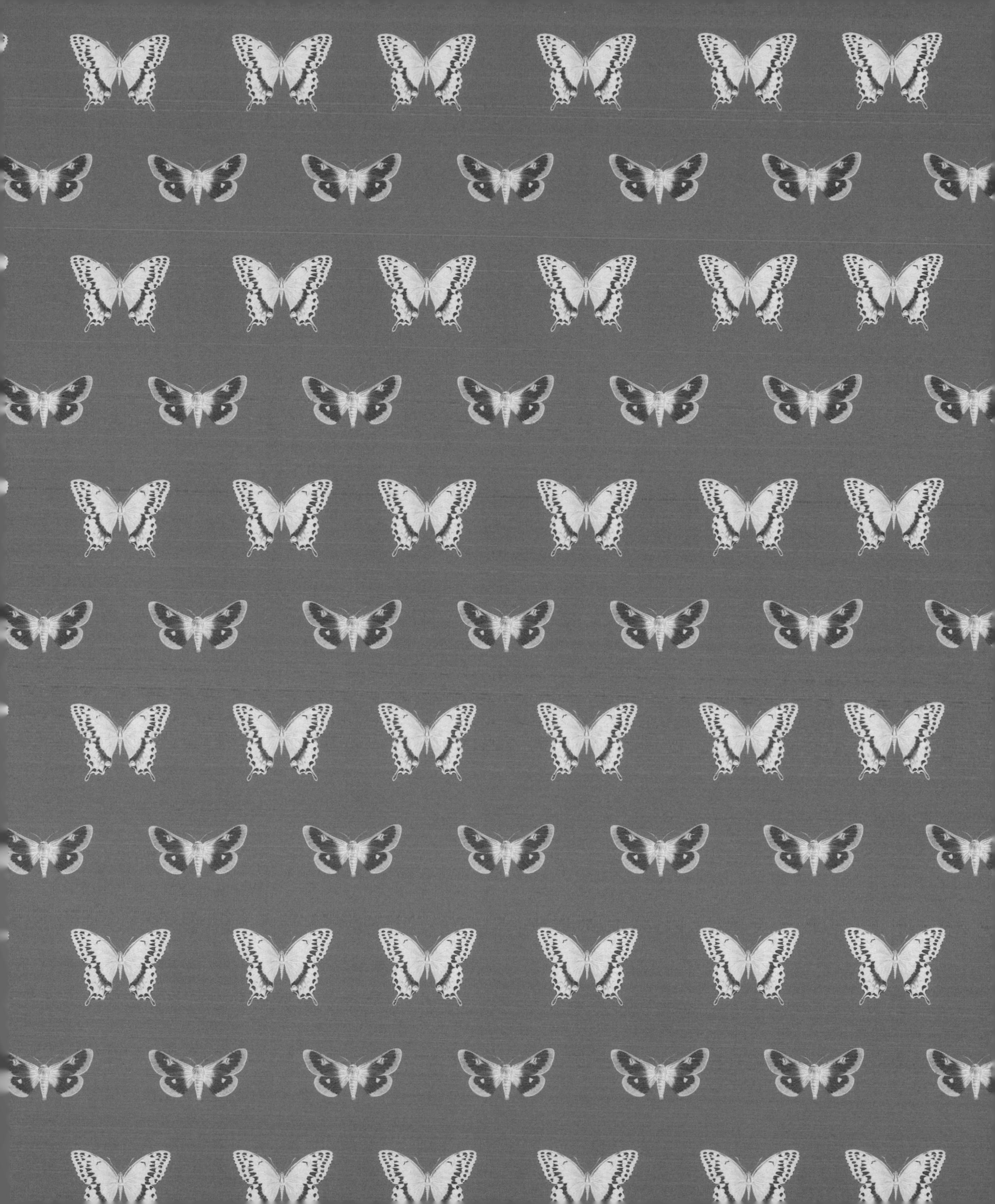

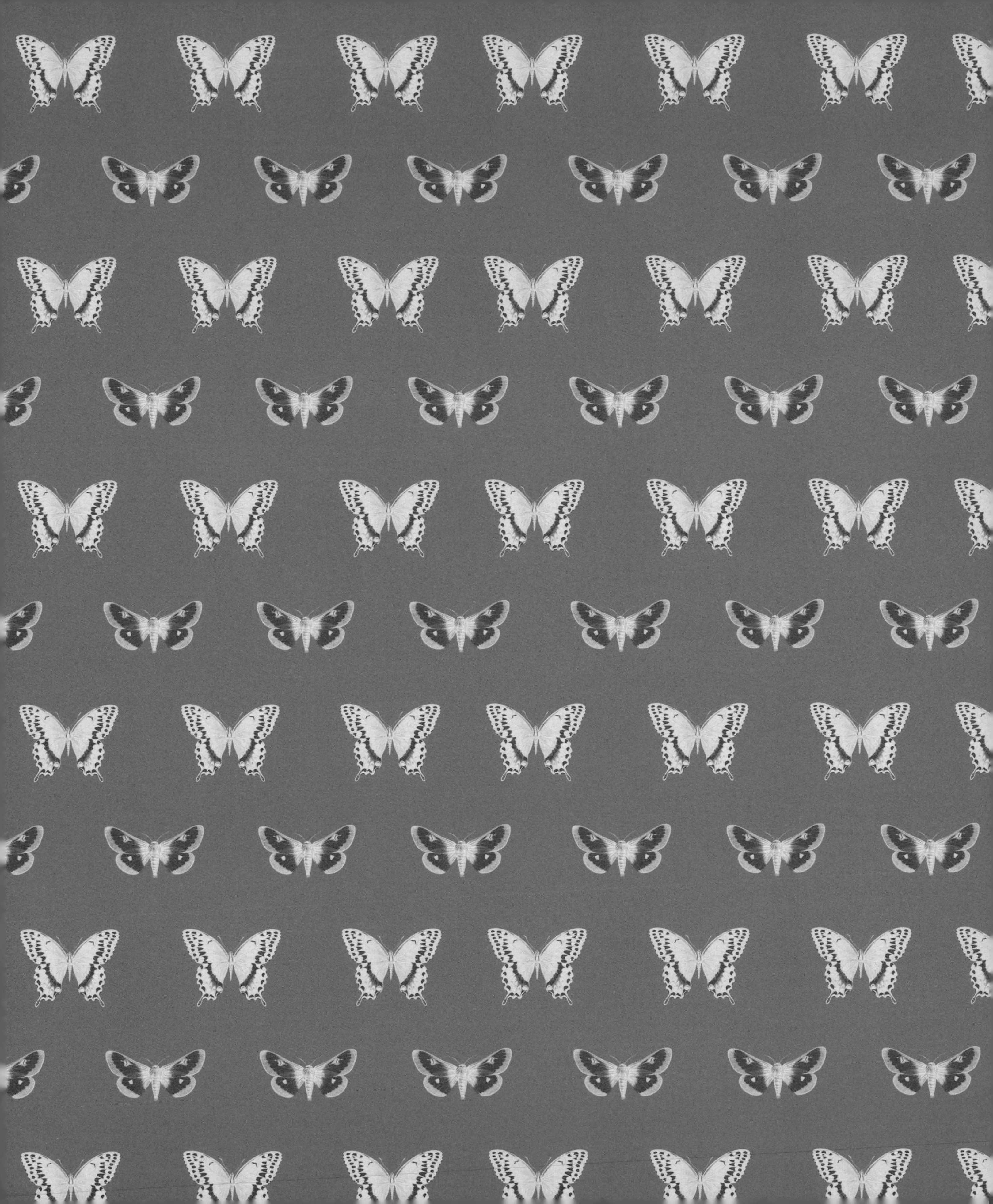

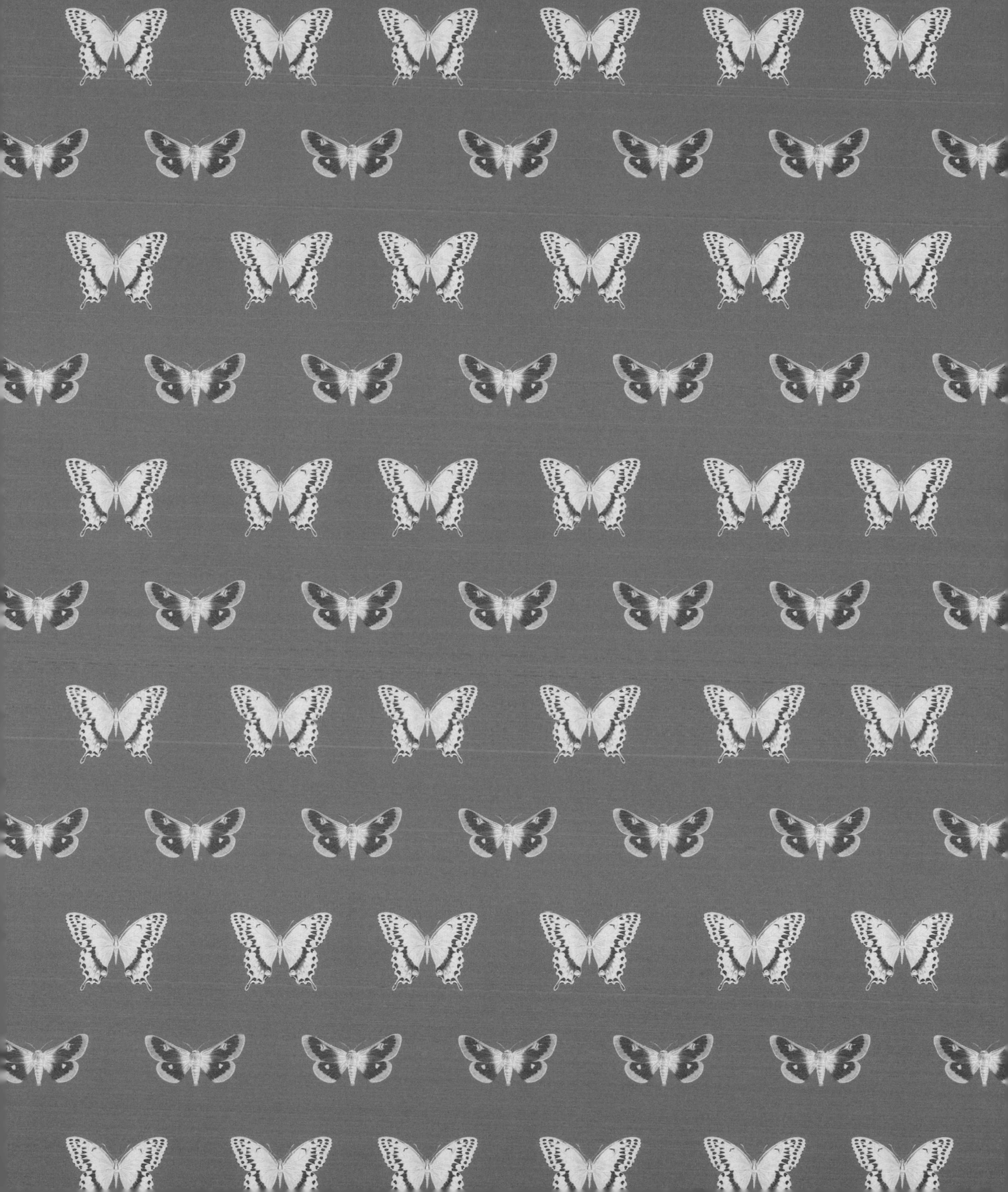

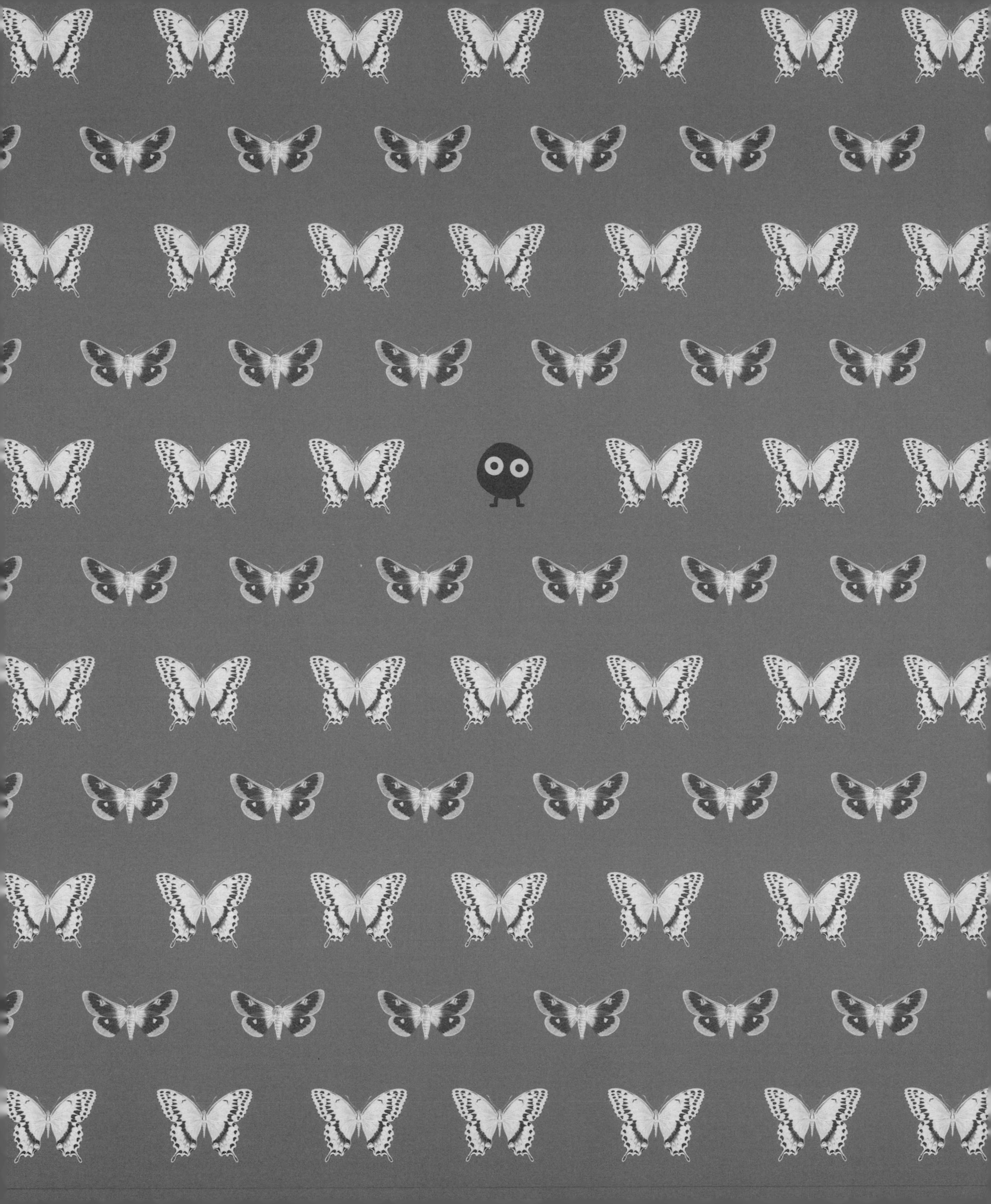